HISTORY'S MOST INFLUENTIAL WRITERS

FROM THE Mid-1900s TO THE 2000s

Pablo Neruda to Toni Morrison

EDITED BY J.E. LUEBERING

Britannica® Educational Publishing

IN ASSOCIATION WITH

ROSEN EDUCATIONAL SERVICES

Published in 2025 by Britannica Educational Publishing
(a trademark of Encyclopædia Britannica, Inc.)
in association with Rosen Educational Services, LLC
2544 Clinton Street, Buffalo, NY 14224.

Distributed exclusively by Rosen Educational Services.
For a listing of additional Britannica Educational Publishing titles, call toll free (800) 237-9932.

First Edition

Britannica Educational Publishing
Michael I. Levy: Executive Editor
Marilyn L. Barton: Senior Coordinator, Production Control
Steven Bosco: Director, Editorial Technologies
Lisa S. Braucher: Senior Producer and Data Editor
Yvette Charboneau: Senior Copy Editor
Kathy Nakamura: Manager, Media Acquisition
J. E. Luebering: Manager and Senior Editor, Literature

Editor: Greg Roza
Book design: Michael Flynn

Photo credits: Cover https://commons.m.wikimedia.org/wiki/File:Toni_Morrison_(author,_at_her_upstate_New_York_home).jpg; p. 7 https://commons.wikimedia.org/wiki/File:Pablo_Neruda_1963.jpg; p. 12 https://commons.wikimedia.org/wiki/File:John_Steinbeck_1939_(cropped).jpg; p. 15 https://commons.wikimedia.org/wiki/File:Samuel_Beckett,_Pic,_1.jpg; p. 19 https://commons.wikimedia.org/wiki/File:Richard_Wright.jpg; p. 21 Chad Robertson Media/Shutterstock.com; p. 25 https://commons.wikimedia.org/wiki/File:Nagib_Machfus_Statue.jpg; p. 27 https://commons.wikimedia.org/wiki/File:Albert_Camus,_gagnant_de_prix_Nobel,_portrait_en_buste,_pos%C3%A9_au_bureau,_faisant_face_%C3%A0_gauche,_cigarette_de_tabagisme.jpg; p. 31 https://commons.wikimedia.org/wiki/File:De_schrijver_staat_de_pers_te_woord,_Bestanddeelnr_927-0019.jpg; p. 35 https://commons.wikimedia.org/wiki/File:Kerouac_by_Palumbo_2_(cropped).png; p. 43 lev radin/Shutterstock.com; p. 47 360b/Shutterstock.com; p. 48 Markus Wissmann/Shutterstock.com; p. 51Fred Duval/Shutterstock.com; p. 52 Mashka/Shutterstock.com; p. 54 Olga Besnard/Shutterstock.com; p. 56 Rena Schild/Shutterstock.com.

Cataloging-in-Publication Data

Names: Luebering, J.E.
Title: From the mid-1900s to the 2000s: Pablo Neruda to Toni Morrison / edited by J.E. Luebering.
Description: New York : Britannica Educational Publishing, in Association with Rosen Educational Services, 2025. | Series: History's most influential writers | Includes glossary and index.
Identifiers: ISBN 9781641901178 (library bound) | ISBN 9781641901161 (pbk) | ISBN 9781641901185 (ebook)
Subjects: LCSH: Authors--20th century--Biography. | Authorship--History--20th century. | Literature, Modern--20th century--Bio-bibliography.
Classification: LCC PN451.F766 2025 | DDC 809'.04 B --dc23

Manufactured in the United States of America

CPSIA Compliance Information: Batch #CSBRIT25. For further information contact Rosen Publishing at 1-800-237-9932.

CONTENTS

Introduction

"If there's a book that you want to read, but it hasn't been written yet, then you must write it."
—Toni Morrison (1931–2019)

Open a book—any book. In it you'll find words, of course, but look closely and you'll also find art, crafted, in detail, by a writer proud enough to sign his or her name to the work. In a book, or in any piece of writing, words are joined together at the whim of the author. Sentences are created, paragraphs and stanzas formatted, chapters built, and stories told. In a book or a poem, a play or a short story, everything is there, on the page, for a reason: to show, to tell, to convey a message.

As the title of this book indicates, all those featured in this collection are influential. Through their work, they've reached out to the masses, touched the hearts and souls of millions, and left their mark on the world. But how exactly is influence defined in this case? Perhaps it's the ability of one person, through his or her writing, to change the way the world thinks. Jack Kerouac is a prime example. Kerouac, an American writer and the literary leader of the so-called Beat Generation, achieved instant fame when his second novel, *On the Road*, was published in 1957. Kerouac typed the book on one long scroll of paper. *On the Road* captures readers' imaginations, takes them for a ride, spins them around, and makes them dizzy. It paints a picture of America like no other novel before it.

Prize-winning authors, whose mastery of language and storytelling is acknowledged by prestigious literary organizations, may be considered highly influential as well. Toni Morrison is the author of the books *Song of Solomon*, (1977) which won the National Book Critics Circle Award for

Fiction, and *Beloved* (1987), which won the Pulitzer Prize for Fiction. In 1993, Morrison became the first Black woman to win the Nobel Prize in Literature.

But Morrison's influence extends well beyond awards and honors. Through her novels, she reached and influenced millions on a personal, socially conscious level. She made readers think about issues facing society, about the implications of racism in America and the struggle that Black people and women—and Black women in particular—continue to go through to secure their place in an often hostile world.

The same holds for Richard Wright, who brought protest fiction to the fore as an American literary movement. Protest fiction is that which tackles social injustice; in this case, racism. At a time when many publishing houses were reluctant to distribute books by or about Black authors, Wright succeeded in getting first *Native Son* (1940), then *Black Boy* (1945), onto shelves and into readers' hands. Wright's success paved the way for future generations of Black writers, which, in turn, helped strengthen the resolve of those in the civil rights movement.

The truth is, influence can mean so many things and can be measured in so many ways. Those who read the works of any of the writers profiled in this book may very well discover an experience they've perhaps never had before. They might have their imagination sparked and be transported, however briefly, from the travails of the life they're living. An author's writing might, with its insight, highlight an injustice, leading readers to speak out themselves and demand an equitable resolution. Whatever the case, one can't read a work by authors such as those detailed here without being influenced in some way. That's the power of great writing. And that's the real reason we read.

PABLO NERUDA

(b. July 12, 1904, Parral, Chile—d. Sept. 23, 1973, Santiago)

Pablo Neruda, a Chilean poet, diplomat, and politician, was awarded the Nobel Prize for Literature in 1971. He was perhaps the most important Latin American poet of the 20th century.

Born Neftalí Ricardo Reyes Basoalto, Neruda began to write poetry at age 10. His father tried to discourage him from writing, which was probably why the young poet began to publish under the pseudonym Pablo Neruda, which he was legally to adopt in 1946. Neruda first published his poems in the local newspapers and later in magazines published in the Chilean capital, Santiago. In 1921 he moved to Santiago to continue his studies and become a French teacher.

His first book of poems, *Crepusculario*, was published in 1923. His second book, *Veinte poemas de amor y una canción desesperada* (1924; *Twenty Love Poems and a Song of Despair*), was inspired by an unhappy love affair. It became an instant success and is still one of Neruda's most popular books. The verse in *Twenty Love Poems* is vigorous, poignant, and direct, yet subtle and very original in its imagery and metaphors. The poems express young, passionate, unhappy love perhaps better than any book of poetry in the long Romantic tradition.

More collections followed, but his poetry was not a steady source of income. He managed to get himself appointed honorary consul to Rangoon in Burma (now Yangôn, Myanmar), and for the next five years he represented his country in Asia. He continued to live in abject poverty, however, since as honorary consul he received

Pablo Neruda (1904–1973) was one of most famous poets of the 20th century.

no salary, and he was tormented by loneliness.

From Rangoon Neruda moved to Colombo in Ceylon (now Sri Lanka). He increasingly came to identify with the South Asian masses, who were heirs to ancient cultures but were downtrodden by poverty, colonial rule, and political oppression. It was during these years in Asia that he wrote *Residencia en la tierra, 1925–1931* (1933; *Residence on Earth*). In this book Neruda moves beyond the lucid, conventional lyricism of *Twenty Love Poems*, abandoning normal syntax, rhyme, and stanzaic organization to create a highly personalized poetic technique. His personal and collective anguish gives rise to nightmarish visions of disintegration, chaos, decay, and death that he recorded in a cryptic, difficult style inspired by Surrealism.

In 1930 Neruda was named consul in Batavia (modern Jakarta), which was then the capital of the Dutch East Indies (now Indonesia). In 1932 Neruda returned to Chile, but he still could not earn a living from his poetry. In 1933 he was appointed Chilean consul in Buenos Aires, Argentina. In 1934 Neruda took up an appointment as consul in Barcelona, Spain, and soon he was transferred to the consulate in Madrid, where he moved ever closer to communism.

A second, enlarged edition of the *Residencia* poems entitled *Residencia en la tierra, 1925–35* was published in two volumes in 1935. In this edition, Neruda begins to move away from the highly personal, often hermetic poetry of the first *Residencia* volume, adopting a more extroverted outlook and a clearer, more accessible style in order to better communicate his new social concerns to the reader.

After supporting the Republicans in the Spanish Civil War, Neruda returned to Chile in 1937 and entered his country's political life, giving lectures and poetry readings while also defending Republican Spain and Chile's new center-left government. In 1939 he was appointed special consul in Paris, where he supervised the migration to Chile of many defeated Spanish Republicans who had escaped to France. In 1940 he took up a post as Chile's consul general in Mexico. He also began work on a long poem, *Canto general* (1950; "General Song," Eng. trans. *Canto general*), that he would complete only after being driven into exile from Chile, after the government he had supported as a member of the Communist Party turned toward the right. Resonant with historical and epic overtones, this epic poem celebrates Latin America—its flora, its fauna, and its history, particularly the wars of liberation from Spanish rule and the continuing struggle of its peoples to obtain freedom and social justice. It also, however, celebrates Joseph Stalin, the bloody Soviet dictator in power at the time. The poem would become one of his key works.

In 1952 the political situation in Chile once again became favorable, and Neruda was able to return home. By that time his works had been translated into many languages, and he was rich and famous. One of his major works, *Odas elementales* (*Elemental Odes*), was published in 1954. Its verse was written in a new poetic style—simple, direct, precise, and humorous—and it contained descriptions of everyday objects, situations, and beings (e.g., *Ode to the Onion* and *Ode to the Cat*). Neruda's poetic output during these years was stimulated by his international fame and personal happiness; 20 books of his appeared between 1958 and his death in 1973, and 8 more were published posthumously. While already ill with cancer in France, Neruda in 1971 learned that he had been awarded the Nobel Prize for Literature. After traveling to Stockholm to receive his prize, he returned to Chile bedridden and terminally ill.

JOHN STEINBECK

(b. Feb. 27, 1902, Salinas, Calif., U.S.—d. Dec. 20, 1968, New York, N.Y.)

The American novelist John Steinbeck is best known for *The Grapes of Wrath* (1939), which summed up the bitterness of the Great Depression decade and aroused widespread sympathy for the plight of migratory farm workers. He received the Nobel Prize for Literature for 1962.

Steinbeck attended Stanford University in California intermittently between 1920 and 1926, but did not take a degree. Before his books attained success, he spent considerable time supporting himself as a manual laborer while writing, and his experiences lent authenticity to his depictions of the lives of the workers in his stories. He spent much of his life in Monterey County, Calif., which later was the setting of some of his fiction.

Steinbeck's first novel, *Cup of Gold* (1929), was followed by *The Pastures of Heaven* (1932) and *To a God Unknown* (1933), none of which were successful. He first achieved popularity with *Tortilla Flat* (1935), an affectionately told story of Mexican-Americans. The mood of gentle humor turned to one of unrelenting grimness in his next novel, *In Dubious Battle* (1936), a classic account of a strike by agricultural laborers and a pair of Marxist labor organizers who engineer it. The novella *Of Mice and Men* (1937), which also appeared in play and film versions, is a tragic story about the strange, complex bond between two migrant laborers.

The Grapes of Wrath won a Pulitzer Prize and a National Book Award and was made into a notable film in 1940. The novel is about the migration of a dispossessed family from the Oklahoma Dust Bowl to California and describes their subsequent exploitation by a ruthless system of agricultural economics. A protest novel punctuated by prose-poem interludes, *The Grapes of Wrath* tells of the Joad family's almost biblical journey, during which they learn the necessity for collective action among the poor and downtrodden to prevent them from being destroyed individually.

After the best-selling success of *The Grapes of Wrath*, Steinbeck went to Mexico to collect marine life with the freelance biologist Edward F. Ricketts, and the two men collaborated in writing *Sea of Cortez* (1941), a study of the fauna of the Gulf of California. During World War II Steinbeck wrote some effective pieces of government propaganda, among them *The Moon Is Down* (1942), a novel of Norwegians under the Nazis. He also served as a war correspondent. His immediate postwar work—*Cannery Row* (1945), *The Pearl* (1947), and *The Wayward Bus* (1947)—contained the familiar elements of his social criticism but were more relaxed in approach and sentimental in tone.

Steinbeck's later writings were comparatively slight

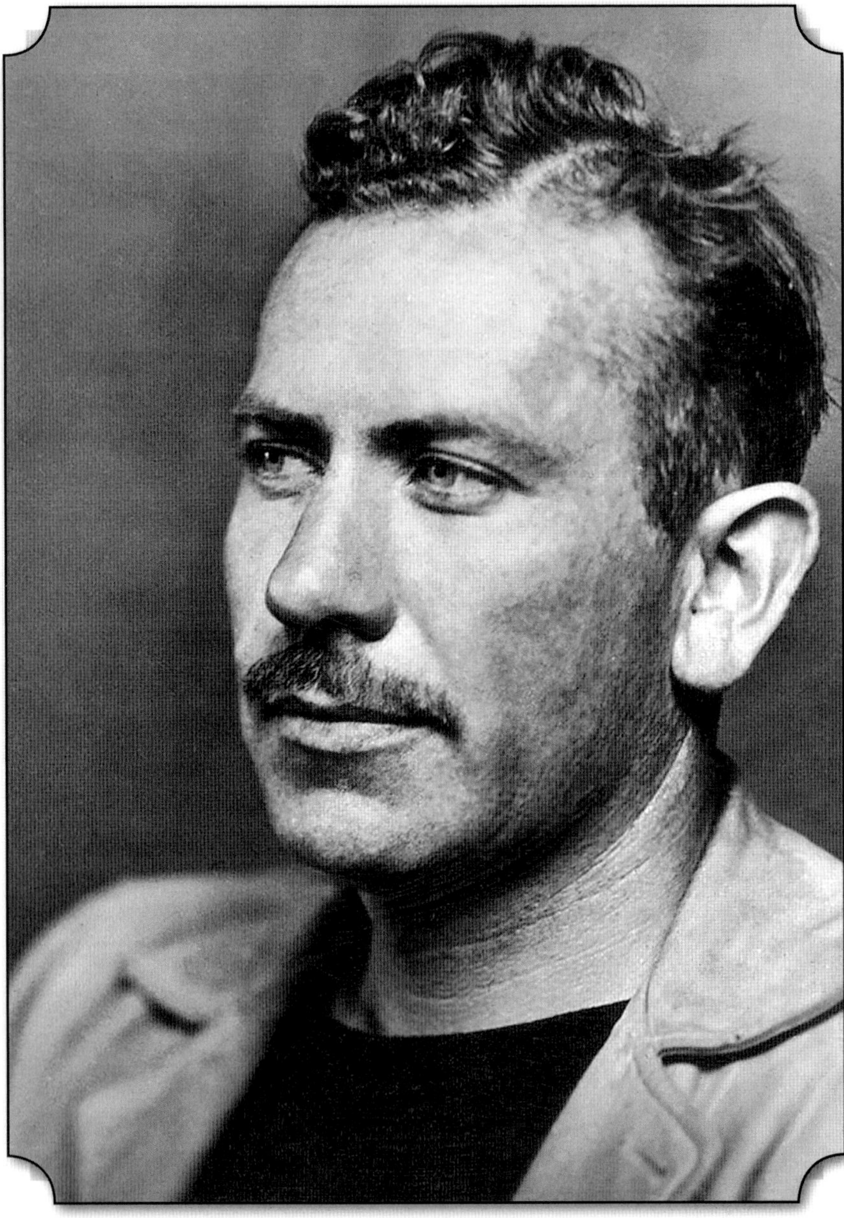

John Steinbeck (1902–1968) was a Nobel Prize winner and an influential writer of American fiction.

works of entertainment and journalism interspersed with three conscientious attempts to reassert his stature as a major novelist: *Burning Bright* (1950), *East of Eden* (1952), and *The Winter of Our Discontent* (1961). In critical opinion, none equaled his earlier achievement. *East of Eden*, an ambitious epic about the moral relations between a California farmer and his two sons, was made into a film in 1955. Steinbeck himself wrote the scripts for the film versions of his stories *The Pearl* (1948) and *The Red Pony* (1949). Outstanding among the scripts he wrote directly for motion pictures were *Forgotten Village* (1941) and *Viva Zapata!* (1952).

Steinbeck's reputation rests mostly on the naturalistic novels with proletarian themes he wrote in the 1930s. It is in these works that his building of rich symbolic structures and his attempts at conveying mythopoeic and archetypal qualities in his characters are most effective.

SAMUEL BECKETT

(b. April 13?, 1906, Foxrock, County Dublin, Ire.—d. Dec. 22, 1989, Paris, France)

Author, critic, and playwright Samuel Beckett was the winner of the Nobel Prize for Literature in 1969. He wrote in both French and English and is perhaps best known for his plays, especially *En attendant Godot* (1952; *Waiting for Godot*).

Beckett was born in a suburb of Dublin. Like his fellow Irish writers George Bernard Shaw, Oscar Wilde, and William Butler Yeats, he came from a Protestant, Anglo-Irish background. At the age of 14 he went to the Portora

Royal School, in what became Northern Ireland, a school that catered to the Anglo-Irish middle classes.

From 1923 to 1927, he studied Romance languages at Trinity College, Dublin, where he received his bachelor's degree. After a brief spell of teaching in Belfast, he became a reader in English at the École Normale Supérieure in Paris in 1928. There he met the self-exiled Irish writer James Joyce, the author of the controversial and seminally modern novel *Ulysses*, and joined his circle. Contrary to often-repeated reports, however, he never served as Joyce's secretary. He returned to Ireland in 1930 to take up a post as lecturer in French at Trinity College, but after only four terms he resigned, in December 1931, and embarked upon a period of restless travel in London, France, Germany, and Italy.

In 1937 Beckett decided to settle in Paris. As a citizen of a country that was neutral in World War II, he was able to remain there even after the occupation of Paris by the Germans, but he joined an underground resistance group in 1941. When, in 1942, he received news that members of his group had been arrested by the Gestapo, he immediately went into hiding and eventually moved to the unoccupied zone of France. Until the liberation of the country, he supported himself as an agricultural laborer. In 1945 he returned to Ireland but volunteered for the Irish Red Cross and went back to France as an interpreter in a military hospital in Saint-Lô, Normandy. In the winter of 1945, he finally returned to Paris and was awarded the Croix de Guerre for his resistance work.

There followed a period of intense creativity, the

Samuel Beckett (1906–1989) was an Irish writer of novels, short stories, plays, and poems.

most concentratedly fruitful period of Beckett's life. His relatively few prewar publications included two essays on Joyce and the French novelist Marcel Proust. The volume *More Pricks Than Kicks* (1934) contained 10 stories describing episodes in the life of a Dublin intellectual, Belacqua Shuah, and the novel *Murphy* (1938) concerns an Irishman in London who escapes from a girl he is about to marry to a life of contemplation as a male nurse in a mental institution. His two slim volumes of poetry were *Whoroscope* (1930), a poem on the French philosopher René Descartes, and the collection *Echo's Bones* (1935). A number of short stories and poems were scattered in various periodicals. He wrote the novel *Dream of Fair to Middling Women* in the mid-1930s, but it remained incomplete and was not published until 1992.

During his years in hiding in unoccupied France, Beckett also completed another novel, *Watt*, which was not published until 1953. After his return to Paris, between 1946 and 1949, Beckett produced a number of stories, the major prose narratives *Molloy* (1951), *Malone meurt* (1951; *Malone Dies*), and *L'Innommable* (1953; *The Unnamable*), and two plays, the unpublished three-act *Eleutheria* and *Waiting for Godot*.

It was not until 1951, however, that these works saw the light of day. After many refusals, Suzanne Deschevaux-Dumesnil (later Mme Beckett), Beckett's lifelong companion, finally succeeded in finding a publisher for *Molloy*. When this book not only proved a modest commercial success but also was received with enthusiasm by the French critics, the same publisher brought out the two other novels and *Waiting for Godot*. It was with the amazing success of *Waiting for Godot* at the small Théâtre de Babylone in Paris, in January 1953, that Beckett's rise to world fame began. Beckett continued writing, but more slowly than in the immediate postwar years. Plays for the stage and radio and a number of prose works occupied much of his attention.

Beckett continued to live in Paris, but most of his writing was done in a small house secluded in the Marne valley, a short drive from Paris. His total dedication to his art extended to his complete avoidance of all personal publicity, of appearances on radio or television, and of all journalistic interviews. When, in 1969, he received the Nobel Prize for Literature, he accepted the award but declined the trip to Stockholm to avoid the public speech at the ceremonies.

In spite of Beckett's courageous tackling of the ultimate mystery and despair of human existence, he was essentially a comic writer. Far from being gloomy and depressing, the ultimate effect of seeing or reading Beckett is one of cathartic release, an objective as old as theater itself.

RICHARD WRIGHT

(b. Sept. 4, 1908, near Natchez, Miss., U.S.—d. Nov. 28, 1960, Paris, France)

The novelist and short-story writer Richard Wright was among the first Black American writers to protest white treatment of Blacks, notably in his novel *Native Son* (1940) and his autobiography, *Black Boy* (1945). He inaugurated the tradition of protest explored by other Black writers after World War II.

Wright's grandparents had been enslaved. His father left home when he was five, and the boy, who grew up in poverty, was often shifted from one relative to another. He worked at a number of jobs before joining the northward migration, first to Memphis, Tenn., and then to Chicago. There, after working in unskilled jobs, he got an opportunity to write through the Federal Writers' Project. In 1932 he became a member of the Communist Party, and in 1937 he went to New York City, where he became Harlem editor of the Communist *Daily Worker*.

Wright first came to the general public's attention with a volume of novellas, *Uncle Tom's Children* (1938), based on the question: How may a Black man live in a country that denies his humanity? In each story but one the hero's quest ends in death. His fictional scene shifted to Chicago in *Native Son*. Its protagonist, a poor Black youth named Bigger Thomas, accidentally kills a white girl, and in the course of his ensuing flight his hitherto meaningless awareness of antagonism from a white world becomes intelligible. The book was a best-seller and was staged successfully as a play on Broadway (1941) by Orson Welles. Wright himself played Bigger Thomas in a motion-picture version made in Argentina in 1951.

In 1944 Wright left the Communist Party because of political and personal differences. *Black Boy*, written a year later, is a moving account of his childhood and young manhood in the South. The book chronicles the extreme poverty of his childhood, his experience of white prejudice and violence against Blacks, and his growing awareness of his interest in literature.

After World War II, Wright settled in Paris as a

The literary works of Richard Wright (1908–1960) focused on the challenges faced by African Americans.

permanent expatriate. *The Outsider* (1953), acclaimed as the first American existential novel, warned that the Black man had awakened in a disintegrating society not ready to include him. Three later novels were not well-received. Among his polemical writings of that period was *White Man, Listen!* (1957), which was originally a series of lectures given in Europe. *Eight Men*, a collection of short stories, appeared in 1961.

The autobiographical *American Hunger*, which narrates Wright's experiences after moving to the North, was published posthumously in 1977. Some of the more candid passages dealing with race, sex, and politics in Wright's books had been cut or omitted before original publication. Unexpurgated versions of *Native Son*, *Black Boy*, and his other works were published in 1991, however.

EUDORA WELTY

(b. April 13, 1909, Jackson, Miss., U.S.—d. July 23, 2001, Jackson)

Eudora Welty was an American short-story writer and novelist whose work is mainly focused with great precision on the regional manners of people inhabiting a small Mississippi town that resembles her own birthplace and the Delta country.

Welty attended Mississippi State College for Women before transferring to the University of Wisconsin, from which she graduated in 1929. During the Great Depression she was a photographer on the Works Progress Administration's Guide to Mississippi, and photography remained a lifelong interest. *Photographs* (1989) is a collection of many of the photographs she

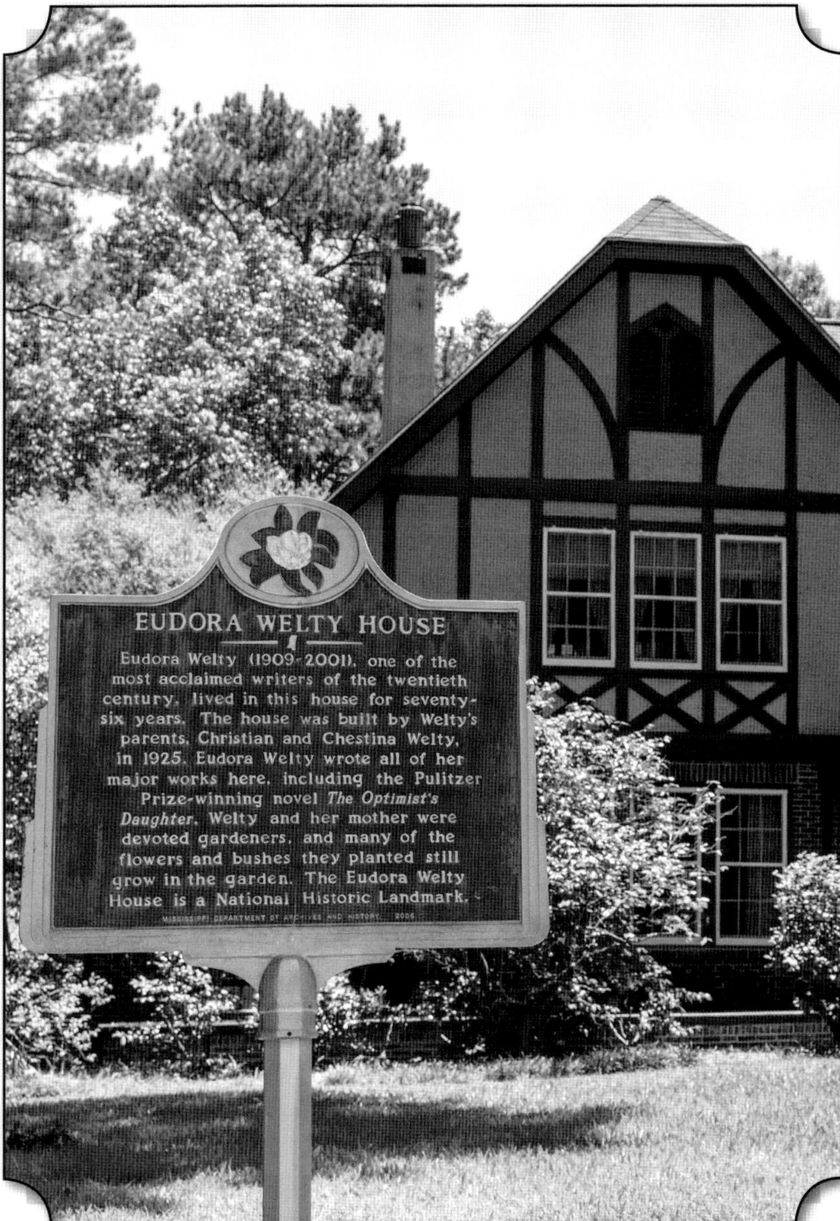

Eudora Welty's house in Jackson, Mississippi, is registered as a National Historic Landmark.

took for the WPA. She also worked as a writer for a radio station and newspaper in her native Jackson, Mississippi, before her fiction won popular and critical acclaim.

Welty's first short story was published in 1936, and thereafter her work began to appear regularly, first in little magazines such as the *Southern Review* and later in major periodicals such as *The Atlantic Monthly* and *The New Yorker*. Her readership grew steadily after the publication of *A Curtain of Green* (1941; enlarged 1979), a volume of short stories that contains two of her most anthologized stories, "The Petrified Man" and "Why I Live at the P.O." In 1942 her short novel *The Robber Bridegroom* was issued, and in 1946 her first full-length novel, *Delta Wedding*. Her later novels include *The Ponder Heart* (1954), *Losing Battles* (1970), and *The Optimist's Daughter* (1972), which won a Pulitzer Prize. *The Wide Net and Other Stories* (1943), *The Golden Apples* (1949), and *The Bride of Innisfallen and Other Stories* (1955) are collections of short stories, and *The Eye of the Story* (1978) is a volume of essays. *The Collected Stories of Eudora Welty* was published in 1980.

Welty's main subject is the intricacies of human relationships, particularly as revealed through her characters' interactions in intimate social encounters. Among her themes are the subjectivity and ambiguity of people's perception of character and the presence of virtue hidden beneath an obscuring surface of convention, insensitivity, and social prejudice. Welty's outlook is hopeful, and love is viewed as a redeeming presence in the midst of isolation and indifference. Her works combine humor and psychological acuity with a sharp ear for regional speech patterns.

One Writer's Beginnings, an autobiographical work, was published in 1984. Originating in a series of three lectures given at Harvard, it beautifully evoked what Welty styled her "sheltered life" in Jackson and how her early fiction grew out of it.

NAGUIB MAHFOUZ

(b. Dec. 11, 1911, Cairo, Egypt—d. Aug. 30, 2006, Cairo)

The Egyptian novelist and screenplay writer Naguid Mahfouz was awarded the Nobel Prize for Literature in 1988, the first Arabic writer to be so honored.

Mahfouz was the son of a civil servant and grew up in Cairo's Al-Jamāliyyah district. He attended Fu'ād I University (now Cairo University), where in 1934 he received a degree in philosophy. He worked in the Egyptian civil service in a variety of positions from 1934 until his retirement in 1971.

Mahfouz's earliest published works were short stories. His early novels, such as *Rādūbīs* (1943; "Radobis"), were set in ancient Egypt, but he had turned to describing modern Egyptian society by the time he began his major work, *Al-Thulāthiyyah* (1956–57), known as *The Cairo Trilogy*. Its three novels—*Bayn al-qasrayn* (1956; *Palace Walk*), *Qaṣr al-shawq* (1957; *Palace of Desire*), and *Al-Sukkariyyah* (1957; *Sugar Street*)—depict the lives of three generations of different families in Cairo from World War I until after the 1952 military coup that overthrew King Farouk. The trilogy provides a penetrating overview of 20th-century Egyptian thought, attitudes, and social change.

In subsequent works Mahfouz offered critical views of the old Egyptian monarchy, British colonialism, and contemporary Egypt. Several of his more notable novels deal with social issues involving women and political prisoners. His novel *Awlād ḥāratinā* (1959; *Children of the Alley*) was banned in Egypt for a time because of its controversial treatment of religion and its use of characters based on Muhammad, Moses, and other figures. Islamic militants, partly because of their outrage over the work, later called for his death, and in 1994 Mahfouz was stabbed in the neck.

Mahfouz's other novels include *Al-Liṣṣ wa-al-kilāb* (1961; *The Thief and the Dogs*), *Al-Shaḥḥādh* (1965; *The Beggar*), and *Mīrāmār* (1967; *Miramar*), all of which consider Egyptian society under Gamal Abdel Nasser's regime; *Afrāḥ al-qubba* (1981; *Wedding Song*), set among several characters associated with a Cairo theater company; and the structurally experimental *Ḥadīth al-ṣabāḥ wa-al-masā'* (1987; *Morning and Evening Talk*), which strings together in alphabetical order dozens of character sketches. Together, his novels, which were among the first to gain widespread acceptance in the Arabic-speaking world, brought the genre to maturity within Arabic literature.

Mahfouz's achievements as a short-story writer are demonstrated in such collections as *Dunyā Allāh* (1963; *God's World*). *The Time and the Place, and Other Stories* (1991) and *The Seventh Heaven* (2005) are collections of his stories in English translation. Mahfouz wrote more than 45 novels and short-story collections, as well as some 30 screenplays and several plays. *Asdā' al-sīrah al-dhātiyyah*

A statue commemorates Naguib Mahfouz, Egyptian author of more than 30 novels and 350 short stories.

(1996; *Echoes of an Autobiography*) is a collection of parables and his sayings. In 1996 the Naguib Mahfouz Medal for Literature was established to honor Arabic writers.

ALBERT CAMUS

(b. Nov. 7, 1913, Mondovi, Alg.—d. Jan. 4, 1960, near Sens, France)

The French novelist, essayist, and playwright Albert Camus was best known for such novels as *L'Étranger* (1942; *The Stranger*), *La Peste* (1947; *The Plague*), and *La Chute* (1956; *The Fall*) and for his work in leftist causes. He received the 1957 Nobel Prize for Literature.

While attending the University of Algiers, Camus was particularly influenced by one of his teachers, Jean Grenier, who helped him to develop his literary and philosophical ideas. He obtained a *diplôme d'études supérieures* in 1936 for a thesis on the relationship between Greek and Christian thought in the philosophical writings of Plotinus and St. Augustine. His candidature for the *agrégation* (a qualification that would have enabled him to take up a university career) was cut short, however, by an attack of tuberculosis. To regain his health he went to a resort in the French Alps—his first visit to Europe—and eventually returned to Algiers via Florence, Pisa, and Genoa.

Throughout the 1930s, Camus broadened his interests. He read the French classics as well as the writers of the day—among them André Gide, Henry de Montherlant, André Malraux—and was a prominent figure among the young left-wing intellectuals of Algiers. For a short period in 1934–35 he was also a member of the Algerian Communist Party. In addition, he wrote,

Albert Camus (1913–1960) was a French philosopher, author, and activist.

produced, adapted, and acted for the Théâtre du Travail (Workers' Theater, later named the Théâtre de l'Équipe), which aimed to bring outstanding plays to working-class audiences. He maintained a deep love of the theater until his death. Ironically, his plays are the least-admired part of his literary output, although *Le Malentendu* (*Cross Purpose*) and *Caligula*, first produced in 1944 and 1945, respectively, remain landmarks in the Theater of the Absurd.

In the two years before the outbreak of World War II, Camus served his apprenticeship as a journalist with *Alger-Républicain* in many capacities. He reviewed some of Jean-Paul Sartre's early literary works and wrote an important series of articles analyzing social conditions among the Muslims of the Kabylie region. These articles, reprinted in abridged form in *Actuelles III* (1958), drew attention (15 years in advance) to many of the injustices that led to the outbreak of the Algerian War in 1954.

He enjoyed the most influence as a journalist during the final years of the occupation of France and the immediate post-Liberation period. As editor of the Parisian daily *Combat*, the successor of a resistance newssheet run largely by Camus, he held an independent left-wing position based on the ideals of justice and truth and the belief that all political action must have a solid moral basis.

By now Camus had become a leading literary figure. *L'Étranger* (*The Stranger*), a brilliant first novel begun before the war and published in 1942, is a study of 20th-century alienation with a portrait of an "outsider" condemned to death less for shooting an Arab than for the fact that he never says more than he genuinely feels and refuses to conform to society's demands. The same year saw the publication of an influential philosophical essay, *Le Mythe de Sisyphe* (*The Myth of Sisyphus*), in which Camus, with considerable sympathy, analyzed contemporary nihilism and a sense of the "absurd." He was already seeking a way of overcoming nihilism, and his second novel, *La Peste* (1947; *The Plague*), is a symbolical account of the fight against an epidemic in Oran by characters whose importance lies less in the (doubtful) success with which they oppose the epidemic than in their determined assertion of human dignity and fraternity. His other major literary works are the technically brilliant novel *La Chute* (1956) and a collection of short stories, *L'Exil et le royaume* (1957; *Exile and the Kingdom*). *La Chute* reveals a preoccupation with Christian symbolism and contains an ironical and witty exposure of the more complacent forms of secular humanist morality.

In 1957, at the early age of 44, Camus received the Nobel Prize for Literature. With characteristic modesty he declared that had he been a member of the awarding committee, his vote would certainly have gone to André Malraux. Less than three years later Camus was killed in an automobile accident.

As novelist and playwright, moralist, and political theorist, Albert Camus after World War II became the spokesman of his own generation and the mentor of the next, not only in France but also in Europe and eventually the world. His writings, which addressed themselves mainly to the isolation of man in an alien universe, the estrangement of the individual from himself, the problem of evil, and the pressing finality of death, accurately reflected the alienation and disillusionment of the post-war intellectual. He is remembered, with Sartre, as a leading practitioner of the existential novel.

ALEKSANDR SOLZHENITSYN

(b. Dec. 11, 1918, Kislovodsk, Russia—d. Aug. 3, 2008, Troitse-Lykovo, near Moscow)

Aleksandr Isayevich Solzhenitsyn, a Russian novelist and historian, was awarded the Nobel Prize for Literature in 1970.

Solzhenitsyn fought in World War II, achieving the rank of captain of artillery; in 1945, however, he was arrested for writing a letter in which he criticized Joseph Stalin and spent eight years in prisons and labor camps, after which he spent three more years in enforced exile. Rehabilitated in 1956, he was allowed to settle in Ryazan, in central Russia, where he became a mathematics teacher and began to write.

Encouraged by the loosening of government restraints on cultural life that was a hallmark of the de-Stalinizing policies of the early 1960s, Solzhenitsyn submitted his short novel *Odin den iz zhizni Ivana Denisovicha* (1962; *One Day in the Life of Ivan Denisovich*) to the leading Soviet literary periodical *Novy Mir* ("New World"). The novel quickly appeared in that journal's pages and met with immediate popularity, Solzhenitsyn becoming an instant celebrity. *Ivan Denisovich*, based on Solzhenitsyn's own experiences, described a typical day in the life of an inmate of a forced-labor camp during the Stalin era. The book produced a political sensation both abroad and in the Soviet Union, where it inspired a

Aleksandr Solzhenitsyn (1918–2008) is best known for his literary depictions of life and political repression in the Soviet Union.

number of other writers to produce accounts of their imprisonment under Stalin's regime.

Solzhenitsyn's period of official favor proved to be short-lived, however. Ideological strictures on cultural activity in the Soviet Union tightened with Nikita Khrushchev's fall from power in 1964, and Solzhenitsyn met first with increasing criticism and then with overt harassment from the authorities when he emerged as an eloquent opponent of repressive government policies. After the publication of a collection of his short stories in 1963, he was denied further official publication of his work, and he resorted to circulating them in the form of *samizdat* ("self-published") literature—i.e., as illegal literature circulated clandestinely—as well as publishing them abroad.

The following years were marked by the foreign publication of several ambitious novels that secured Solzhenitsyn's international literary reputation, among them *Vkruge pervom* (1968; *The First Circle*), which traces the varying responses of scientists at work on research for the secret police as they must decide whether to cooperate with the authorities and thus remain within the research prison or to refuse their services and be thrust back into the brutal conditions of the labor camps.

In 1970 Solzhenitsyn was awarded the Nobel Prize for Literature, but he declined to go to Stockholm to receive the prize for fear he would not be readmitted to the Soviet Union by the government upon his return.

In December 1973 the first parts of *Arkhipelag Gulag* (*The Gulag Archipelago*) were published in Paris after a copy of the manuscript had been seized in the Soviet

Union by the KGB. (*Gulag* is an acronym formed from the official Soviet designation of its system of prisons and labor camps.) *The Gulag Archipelago* is Solzhenitsyn's attempt to compile a literary-historical record of the vast system of prisons and labor camps that came into being shortly after the Bolsheviks seized power in Russia (1917) and that underwent an enormous expansion during the rule of Stalin (1924–53). Various sections of the work describe the arrest, interrogation, conviction, transportation, and imprisonment of the Gulag's victims as practiced by Soviet authorities over four decades. The work mingles historical exposition and Solzhenitsyn's own autobiographical accounts with the voluminous personal testimony of other inmates that he collected and committed to memory during his imprisonment.

Upon publication of the first volume of *The Gulag Archipelago*, Solzhenitsyn was immediately attacked in the Soviet press. Despite the intense interest in his fate that was shown in the West, he was arrested and charged with treason on Feb. 12, 1974. Solzhenitsyn was exiled from the Soviet Union on the following day, and in December he took possession of his Nobel Prize. The second and third volumes of *The Gulag Archipelago* were published in 1974–75. Solzhenitsyn traveled to the United States, where he eventually settled on a secluded estate in Cavendish, Vt.

In presenting alternatives to the Soviet regime, Solzhenitsyn tended to reject Western emphases on democracy and individual freedom and instead favored the formation of a benevolent authoritarian regime that would draw upon the resources of Russia's traditional

Christian values. The introduction of *glasnost* ("openness") in the late 1980s brought renewed access to Solzhenitsyn's work in the Soviet Union. In 1989 the Soviet literary magazine *Novy Mir* published the first officially approved excerpts from *The Gulag Archipelago*. Solzhenitsyn's Soviet citizenship was officially restored in 1990.

Solzhenitsyn ended his exile and returned to Russia in 1994. He subsequently made several public appearances and even met privately with Russian Pres. Boris Yeltsin. Installments of his autobiography, *Ugodilo zernyshko promezh dvukh zhernovov: ocherki izgnaniia* ("The Little Grain Managed to Land Between Two Millstones: Sketches of Exile"), were published from 1998 to 2003. In 2007 Solzhenitsyn was awarded Russia's prestigious State Prize for his contribution to humanitarian causes.

JACK KEROUAC

(b. March 12, 1922, Lowell, Mass., U.S.—d. Oct. 21, 1969, St. Petersburg, Fla.)

Jack Kerouac, an American novelist and poet and the leader of the Beat movement, is best known for his book *On the Road* (1957), which captured the spirit of its time as no other work of the 20th century did.

Kerouac, who spoke joual (a Canadian dialect of French), attended a French Canadian school in Lowell, Mass., in the morning and continued his studies in English in the afternoon. He subsequently went to the Horace Mann School, a preparatory school in New York City, on a football scholarship. In 1940 Kerouac enrolled at Columbia University, where he met two writers who

Jack Kerouac (1922–1969) was a pioneering writer of the Beat Generation.

would become lifelong friends: Allen Ginsberg and William S. Burroughs. Together with Kerouac they are the seminal figures of the Beat movement.

By the time Kerouac and Burroughs met, in 1944, Kerouac had already written a million words. His boyhood ambition had been to write the "great American novel." His first novel, *The Town & the City* (1950), received favorable reviews but was considered derivative of the novels of Thomas Wolfe, whose *Time and the River* (1935) and *You Can't Go Home Again* (1940) were then popular. Yet Kerouac was unhappy with the pace of his prose. The music of bebop jazz artists Thelonious Monk and Charlie Parker began to drive Kerouac toward his "spontaneous bop prosody," as Ginsberg later called it, which took shape in the late 1940s through various drafts of his second novel, *On the Road*. The original manuscript, a scroll written in a three-week blast in 1951, is legendary: composed of approximately 120 feet (37 m) of paper taped together and fed into a manual typewriter, the scroll allowed Kerouac the fast pace he was hoping to achieve. Rejected for publication at first, it finally was printed in 1957. Kerouac found himself a national sensation after *On the Road* received a rave review from *The New York Times*.

Readers often confused Kerouac with Sal Paradise, the amoral hipster at the center of his novel. The critic Norman Podhoretz famously wrote that Beat writing was an assault against the intellect and against decency. This misreading dominated negative reactions to *On the Road*. Through the novel's characterization of hipsters and their nonconformist celebration of sex, jazz, and endless movement, Kerouac wanted to achieve in his writing that which he could find neither in the promise of America nor in the empty spirituality of Roman Catholicism; he strived instead for the serenity that he had discovered in his adopted Buddhism. Kerouac felt that the Beat label marginalized him and prevented him from being treated as he wanted to be treated, as a man of letters in the American tradition of Herman Melville and Walt Whitman.

As he continued to experiment with his prose style, Kerouac also bolstered his standing among the Beat writers as a poet supreme. With his sonnets and odes he ranged across Western poetic traditions. He also experimented with the idioms of blues and jazz in such works as *Mexico City Blues* (1959), a sequential poem comprising 242 choruses. After he met the poet Gary Snyder in 1955, Kerouac's poetry, as well as that of Ginsberg and fellow Beats Philip Whalen and Lew Welch, began to show the influence of the haiku, a genre mostly unknown to Americans at that time.

Kerouac turned to Buddhist study and practice from 1953 to 1956, after his "road" period and in the lull between composing *On the Road* in 1951 and its publication in 1957. In the fall of 1953 he finished *The Subterraneans* (it would be published in 1958). Fed up with the world after the failed love affair upon which the book was based, he read Henry David Thoreau and fantasized a life outside civilization. He immersed himself in the study of Zen.

By the 1960s Kerouac had finished most of the writing for which he is best known. In 1961 he wrote *Big Sur* in 10 days while living in the cabin of Lawrence

Ferlinghetti, a fellow Beat poet, in California's Big Sur region. Another important autobiographical book, *Vanity of Duluoz* (1968), recounts stories of his childhood, his schooling, and the dramatic scandals that defined early Beat legend.

In 1969 Kerouac was broke, and many of his books were out of print. An alcoholic, he was living with his third wife and his mother in St. Petersburg, Fla., where he spent his time in local bars. A week after he had been beaten by fellow drinkers whom he had antagonized, he died of internal hemorrhaging while sitting in front of his television.

FLANNERY O'CONNOR

(b. March 25, 1925, Savannah, Ga., U.S.—d. Aug. 3, 1964, Milledgeville, Ga.)

Flannery O'Connor was an American novelist and short-story writer whose works, usually set in the rural American South and often treating alienation, are concerned with the relationship between the individual and God.

O'Connor grew up in a prominent Roman Catholic family in her native Georgia. She lived in Savannah until her adolescence, but the worsening of her father's lupus erythematosus forced the family to relocate in 1938 to the home in rural Milledgeville where her mother had been raised. After graduating from Georgia State College for Women (now Georgia College & State University) in 1945, she studied creative writing at the University of Iowa Writers' Workshop.

Her first published work, a short story, appeared in

Flannery O'Connor's home in Milledgeville, Georgia, is called Andalusia Farm. It is now open to visitors as a museum.

the magazine *Accent* in 1946. Her first novel, *Wise Blood* (1952; film 1979), explored, in O'Connor's own words, the "religious consciousness without a religion." *Wise Blood* consists of a series of near-independent chapters—many of which originated in previously published short stories—that tell the tale of Hazel Motes, a man who returns home from military service and founds the Church Without Christ, which leads to a series of interactions with the grotesque inhabitants of his hometown. The work combines the keen ear for common speech, caustic religious imagination, and flair for the absurd that were to characterize her subsequent work. With the publication of further short stories, first collected in *A Good Man Is Hard to Find and Other Stories* (1955), she came to be regarded as a master of the form. The collection's eponymous story has become possibly her best-known work. In it O'Connor creates an unexpected agent of salvation in the character of an escaped convict called The Misfit, who kills a quarreling family on vacation in the Deep South.

Her other works of fiction are a novel, *The Violent Bear It Away* (1960), and the short-story collection *Everything That Rises Must Converge* (1965). A collection of occasional prose pieces, *Mystery and Manners*, appeared in 1969. *The Complete Stories*, published posthumously in 1971, contained several stories that had not previously appeared in book form; it won a National Book Award in 1972.

Disabled for more than a decade by the lupus erythematosus she inherited from her father, which eventually proved fatal, O'Connor lived modestly, writing and raising peafowl on her mother's farm at Milledgeville. The posthumous publication of her letters, under the title *The Habit of Being* (1979), and her book reviews and correspondence with local diocesan newspapers, published as *The Presence of Grace and Other Book Reviews* (1983), provided valuable insight into the life and mind of a writer whose works defy conventional categorization. O'Connor's corpus is notable for the seeming incongruity of a devout Catholic whose darkly comic works commonly feature startling acts of violence and unsympathetic, often depraved, characters. She explained the prevalence of brutality in her stories by noting that violence "is strangely capable of returning my characters to reality and preparing them to accept their moment of grace." It is this divine stripping of man's comforts and hubris, along with the attendant degradation of the corporeal, that stands as the most salient feature of O'Connor's work.

WOLE SOYINKA

(b. July 13, 1934, Abeokuta, Nigeria)

Wole Soyinka is a Nigerian playwright and political activist who received the Nobel Prize for Literature in 1986. He sometimes wrote of modern West Africa in a satirical style, but his serious intent and his belief in the evils inherent in the exercise of power usually was evident in his work as well.

A member of the Yoruba people, Soyinka attended Government College and University College in Ibadan before graduating in 1958 with a degree in English from the University of Leeds in England. Upon his return to

Nigeria, he founded an acting company and wrote his first important play, *A Dance of the Forests* (produced 1960; published 1963), for the Nigerian independence celebrations. The play satirizes the fledgling nation by stripping it of romantic legend and by showing that the present is no more a golden age than was the past.

He wrote several plays in a lighter vein, making fun of pompous, Westernized schoolteachers in *The Lion and the Jewel* (first performed in Ibadan, 1959; published 1963) and mocking the clever preachers of upstart prayer-churches who grow fat on the credulity of their parishioners in *The Trials of Brother Jero* (performed 1960; published 1963) and *Jero's Metamorphosis* (1973). But his more serious plays, such as *The Strong Breed* (1963), *Kongi's Harvest* (opened the first Festival of Negro Arts in Dakar, 1966; published 1967), *The Road* (1965), *From Zia, with Love* (1992), and even the parody *King Baabu* (performed 2001; published 2002), reveal his disregard for African authoritarian leadership and his disillusionment with Nigerian society as a whole.

Other notable plays include *Madmen and Specialists* (performed 1970; published 1971), *Death and the King's Horseman* (1975), and *The Beatification of Area Boy* (1995). In these and Soyinka's other dramas, Western elements are skillfully fused with subject matter and dramatic techniques deeply rooted in Yoruba folklore and religion. Symbolism, flashback, and ingenious plotting contribute to a rich dramatic structure. His best works exhibit humor and fine poetic style as well as a gift for irony and satire and for accurately matching the language of his complex characters to their social position and moral

In 1986, Wole Soyinka became the first Black African to win the Nobel Prize for Literature. He's shown here at an event in 2019.

qualities.

From 1960 to 1964, Soyinka was coeditor of *Black Orpheus*, an important literary journal. From 1960 onward he taught literature and drama and headed theater groups at various Nigerian universities, including those of Ibadan, Ife, and Lagos. After winning the Nobel Prize, he also was sought after as a lecturer, and many of his lectures were published—notably the Reith Lectures of 2004, as *Climate of Fear* (2004).

Though he considered himself primarily a playwright, Soyinka also wrote novels—*The Interpreters* (1965) and *Season of Anomy* (1973)—and several volumes of poetry. The latter include *Idanre, and Other Poems* (1967) and *Poems from Prison* (1969; republished as *A Shuttle in the Crypt*, 1972), published together as *Early Poems* (1998); *Mandela's Earth and Other Poems* (1988); and *Samarkand and Other Markets I Have Known* (2002). His verse is characterized by a precise command of language and a mastery of lyric, dramatic, and meditative poetic forms. He wrote a good deal of *Poems from Prison* while he was jailed in 1967–69 for speaking out against the war brought on by the attempted secession of Biafra from Nigeria. *The Man Died* (1972) is his prose account of his arrest and 22-month imprisonment. Soyinka's principal critical work is *Myth, Literature, and the African World* (1976), a collection of essays in which he examines the role of the artist in the light of Yoruba mythology and symbolism. *Art, Dialogue, and Outrage* (1988) is a work on similar themes of art, culture, and society. He continued to address Africa's ills and Western responsibility in *The Open Sore of a Continent* (1996) and *The Burden of Memory, the Muse of Forgiveness* (1999).

Soyinka was the first Black African to be awarded the Nobel Prize for Literature. An autobiography, *Aké: The Years of Childhood*, was published in 1981 and followed by the companion pieces *Ìsarà: A Voyage Around Essay* (1989) and *Ibadan: The Penkelemes Years: A Memoir, 1946–1965* (1994). In 2006 he published another memoir, *You Must Set Forth at Dawn*. In 2005–06 Soyinka served on the Encyclopædia Britannica Editorial Board of Advisors.

SIR SALMAN RUSHDIE

(b. June 19, 1947, Bombay [now Mumbai], India)

Sir Salman Rushdie remains best known as the Anglo-Indian novelist who was condemned to death by leading Iranian Muslim clerics in 1989 for allegedly having blasphemed Islam in his novel *The Satanic Verses*. His case became the focus of an international controversy.

Rushdie was the son of a prosperous Muslim businessman in India. He was educated at Rugby School and the University of Cambridge, receiving an M.A. degree in history in 1968. Throughout most of the 1970s he worked in London as an advertising copywriter, and his first published novel, *Grimus*, appeared in 1975. His next novel, *Midnight's Children* (1981), an allegory about modern India, was an unexpected critical and popular success that won him international recognition. Like Rushdie's subsequent fiction, *Midnight's Children* is an allegorical fable that examines historical and philosophical issues by means of surreal characters, brooding humor, and an effusive and melodramatic prose style.

The novel *Shame* (1983), based on contemporary

politics in Pakistan, was also popular, but Rushdie's fourth novel, *The Satanic Verses*, encountered a different reception. Some of the adventures in this book depict a character modeled on the Prophet Muhammad and portray both him and his transcription of the Qur'ān in a manner that, after the novel's publication in the summer of 1988, drew criticism from Muslim community leaders in Britain, who denounced the novel as blasphemous. Public demonstrations against the book spread to Pakistan in January 1989. On February 14 the spiritual leader of revolutionary Iran, Ayatollah Ruhollah Khomeini, publicly condemned the book and issued a fatwa (legal opinion) against Rushdie; a bounty was offered to anyone who would execute him. He went into hiding under the protection of Scotland Yard, and—although he occasionally emerged unexpectedly, sometimes in other countries—he was compelled to restrict his movements.

Despite the standing death threat, Rushdie continued to write, producing *Imaginary Homelands* (1991), a collection of essays and criticism; the children's novel *Haroun and the Sea of Stories* (1990); the short-story collection *East, West* (1994); and the novel *The Moor's Last Sigh* (1995). In 1998, after nearly a decade, the Iranian government announced it would no longer seek to enforce its fatwa against Rushdie.

Rushdie's subsequent novels include *The Ground Beneath Her Feet* (1999) and *Fury* (2001). *Step Across This Line* (2002) is a collection of essays he wrote between 1992 and 2002 on subjects from the September 11 attacks to *The Wizard of Oz*. *Shalimar the Clown* (2005), a novel

Salman Rushdie became an American citizen in 2016.

Rushdie survived a violent attack in 2022 but lost one eye.

set primarily in the disputed Kashmir region of the Indian subcontinent, examines the nature of terrorism. *The Enchantress of Florence* (2008) is based on a fictionalized account of the Mughal emperor Akbar.

The children's book *Luka and the Fire of Life* (2010) centers on the efforts of Luka—younger brother to the protagonist of *Haroun and the Sea of Stories*—to locate the titular fire and revive his ailing father. *Two Years Eight Months and Twenty-Eight Nights* (2015) depicts the chaos ensuing from a rent in the fabric separating the world of humans from that of the Arabic mythological figures known as jinn. Reveling in folkloric allusion—the title references *The Thousand and One Nights*—the novel unfurls a tapestry of connected stories celebrating the human imagination.

In *The Golden House* (2017), Rushdie explored the immigrant experience in the United States through a wealthy Indian family that settles in New York City in the early 21st century. His next novel, *Quichotte* (2019), was inspired by Cervantes's Don Quixote. *Languages of Truth: Essays 2003–2020* appeared in 2021.

In August 2022 Rushdie was attacked and seriously injured while onstage in Chautauqua, New York. He had been scheduled to give a speech about the United States being a refuge for exiled artists. Rushdie faced a long recovery and ultimately lost one eye. In 2023 he released the acclaimed novel *Victory City*, which was completed before the attack. A work of magic realism, it opens in 14th-century India, where a nine-year-old girl becomes a vessel for a goddess and builds a thriving city known for its egalitarianism. However, greed and religious extremism ultimately lead to its ruination.

Rushdie received the Booker Prize in 1981 for *Midnight's Children*. He subsequently won the Booker of Bookers (1993) and the Best of the Booker (2008). These special prizes were voted on by the public in honor of the prize's 25th and 40th anniversaries, respectively. Rushdie was knighted in 2007, an honor criticized by the Iranian government and Pakistan's parliament.

J. K. ROWLING

(b. July 31, 1965, Chipping Sodbury, near Bristol, Eng.)

The British author J. K. Rowling is the creator of the popular and critically acclaimed Harry Potter series, about a young sorcerer in training.

After graduating from the University of Exeter in 1986, Rowling began working for Amnesty International in London, where she started to write the Harry Potter adventures. In the early 1990s she traveled to Portugal to teach English as a foreign language, but, after a brief marriage and the birth of her daughter, she returned to the United Kingdom, settling in Edinburgh. Living on public assistance between stints as a French teacher, she continued to write.

Rowling's first book in the series, *Harry Potter and the Philosopher's Stone* (1997; also published as *Harry Potter and the Sorcerer's Stone*), was an immediate success, appealing to both children (its intended audience) and adults. Featuring vivid descriptions and an imaginative story line, it followed the adventures of the unlikely hero Harry Potter, a lonely orphan who discovers that he is actually a wizard and enrolls in the Hogwarts School of Witchcraft and Wizardry. The book received numerous

J. K. Rowling is shown here at a 2018 film premiere for an adaptation of one of her novels.

Harry Potter and the Order of the Phoenix *is the fifth book in J. K. Rowling's acclaimed Harry Potter series.*

awards, including the British Book Award. Succeeding volumes—*Harry Potter and the Chamber of Secrets* (1998), *Harry Potter and the Prisoner of Azkaban* (1999), *Harry Potter and the Goblet of Fire* (2000), *Harry Potter and the Order of the Phoenix* (2003), and *Harry Potter and the Half-Blood Prince* (2005)—also were best-sellers, available in more than 200 countries and some 60 languages. The seventh and final installment in the series, *Harry Potter and the Deathly Hallows*, was released in 2007. Other works include the companion books *Fantastic Beasts & Where to Find Them* and *Quidditch Through the Ages*, both of which were published in 2001, with proceeds going to charity.

The Harry Potter series sparked great enthusiasm among children and was credited with generating a new interest in reading. A film version of the first Harry Potter book was released in 2001 and became one of the top-grossing movies in the world. Other volumes were also made into highly successful films. In 2008 Rowling followed her successful Harry Potter series with *The Tales of Beedle the Bard*, a collection of fairy tales.

Rowling was appointed OBE (Officer of the British Empire) in March 2001. In 2009 she was named a chevalier of the French Legion of Honor.

TONI MORRISON

(b. Feb. 18, 1931, Lorain, Ohio, U.S.—d. Aug. 5, 2019, Bronx, N.Y.)

Toni Morrison was an American writer noted for her examination of the Black experience, particularly Black female experience. She received the Nobel Prize for Literature in 1993.

Toni Morrison (1931–2019) was the first Black woman writer awarded the Nobel Prize for Literature.

Morrison, born Chloe Anthony Wofford, grew up in the American Midwest in a family that possessed an intense love of and appreciation for Black culture. Storytelling, songs, and folktales were a deeply formative part of her childhood. She attended Howard University (B.A., 1953) and Cornell University (M.A., 1955). After teaching at Texas Southern University for two years, she taught at Howard from 1957 to 1964. In 1965 she became a fiction editor. From 1984 she taught writing at the State University of New York at Albany, leaving in 1989 to join the faculty of Princeton University.

Morrison's first book, *The Bluest Eye* (1970), is a novel of initiation concerning a victimized adolescent Black girl who is obsessed by white standards of beauty and longs to have blue eyes. In 1973 a second novel, *Sula*, was published; it examines (among other issues) the dynamics of friendship and the expectations for conformity within the community. *Song of Solomon* (1977) is told by a male narrator in search of his identity; its publication brought Morrison to national attention. *Tar Baby* (1981), set on a Caribbean island, explores conflicts of race, class, and sex. The critically acclaimed *Beloved* (1987), which won a Pulitzer Prize for fiction, is based on the true story of a runaway enslaved person who, at the point of recapture, kills her infant daughter in order to spare her a life of slavery. *Jazz* (1992) is a story of violence and passion set in New York City's Harlem during the 1920s. Subsequent novels are *Paradise* (1998), a richly detailed portrait of a Black utopian community in Oklahoma, and *Love* (2003), an intricate family story that reveals the myriad facets of love and its ostensible opposite. *A Mercy*

Toni Morrison (1931–2019) was the first Black woman writer awarded the Nobel Prize for Literature.

(2008) deals with slavery in 17th-century America.

A work of criticism, *Playing in the Dark: Whiteness and the Literary Imagination*, was published in 1992. Many of her essays and speeches were collected in *What Moves at the Margin: Selected Nonfiction* (edited by Carolyn C. Denard), published in 2008. Additionally, Morrison released several children's books, including *Who's Got Game?: The Ant or the Grasshopper?* and *Who's Got Game?: The Lion or the Mouse?*, both written with her son and published in 2003. *Remember* (2004) chronicles the hardships of Black students during the integration of the American public school system; aimed at children, it uses archival photographs juxtaposed with captions speculating on the thoughts of their subjects. She also wrote the libretto for *Margaret Garner* (2005), an opera about the same story that inspired *Beloved*.

The central theme of Morrison's novels is the Black American experience. In an unjust society, her characters struggle to find themselves and their cultural identity. Her use of fantasy, her sinuous poetic style, and her rich interweaving of the mythic gave her stories great strength and texture. In 2010 Morrison was made an officer of the French Legion of Honor. Two years later she was awarded the U.S. Presidential Medal of Freedom.

Glossary

acuity: The ability to see or understand something easily.

alienation: A withdrawing or separation of a person or a person's affections from an object or position of former attachment.

archetypal: The original model on which representations of the same type are based.

Beat movement: An American social and literary movement originating in the 1950s and centred in the bohemian artist communities of California.

blasphemous: Showing disrespect to God or something holy.

cathartic: Producing a release of emotions.

clandestine: Done in secrecy.

disillusionment: The condition of being dissatisfied or defeated in expectation or hope.

egalitarian: Having to do with a social philosophy advocating the removal of inequalities among people.

existential: Rooted in the experience of existence.

expatriate: Someone who has withdrawn from residence in or allegiance to their native country.

juxtapose: To place side by side for comparison.

melodramatic: Having to do with a work (as a movie or play) marked by the exaggerated emotions of the characters and the importance of action and plot.

mythopoeic: Related to the creation of myths.

nihilism: A belief that existence is meaningless.

novella: A short narrative form with its origins in medieval Italy.

posthumous: Taking place after the death of someone.

prose: Writing that is not poetry.

prosody: The rhythmic elements of language.

pseudonym: A pen name.

satire: Something that makes fun of and shows the weaknesses of human nature.

For More Information

BOOKS

Levy, Janey. *Toni Morrison.* New York, NY: Gareth Stevens Publishing, 2021.

Rowling, J. K. *Harry Potter and the Order of the Phoenix*. London, UK: Bloomsbury Children's Books, 2022.

Rushdie, Salman. *Haroun and the Sea of Stories.* New York, NY: Penguin Books, 2020.

Steinbeck, John. *Of Mice and Men.* London, UK: Penguin Classics, 2023.

WEBSITES

Academy of American Poets

poets.org/poet/jack-kerouac

Learn about the life of Jack Kerouac and read some of his Beat poems.

Eudora Welty House and Garden

welty.mdah.ms.gov/

Explore Eudora Welty's former home in Jackson, Mississippi.

The Nobel Prize
www.nobelprize.org/prizes/lists/all-nobel-prizes-in-literature/
This website contains a list of all the writers who have won a Nobel Prize in Literature.

Poetry Foundation
www.poetryfoundation.org/poets/pablo-neruda
This site offers biographical information about Pablo Neruda and a selection of his poetry.

Index